MOVE UP! DON'T GIVE UP! ENDORSEMENTS

D1526447

"If you want to be encouraged, this is the book for you. Thomas Harrison has written a book that will touch your heart, strengthen your spirit, and stretch your mind. I highly recommend it."

Richard Exley
Author of *When You Lose Someone You Love,*
Dancing in the Dark, and *The Letter*
RichardExleyMinistries.org

"Having known Dr. Thomas Harrison for more than 20 years and having experienced his good friendship has been an incalculable blessing in my life. In a time when mentors and fathers seem to be in short supply, here is a man who more than ably fills both assignments--never from a sense of duty--rather, he genuinely loves pastors. I have been waiting for him to write a book like this for quite some time as it embodies who he is. I am excited for him to share what I have received from him for years: Loving encouragement from someone who has been there, fought the battles, and is genuinely interested in your success."

Eric B. Smith
Lead Pastor
Destiny Church
Dayton, Ohio
DestinyDayton.com

"Dr. Thomas Harrison is a prophetic encourager. "One who prophesies strengthens others, encourages them, and comforts them." 1 Corinthians 14:3 (NLT)

Whether he is speaking to a minister's conference, a corporate business setting, or conversing over coffee with a friend, he always shares insight, help, and motivation, and when needed, a recommended course-correction. I have seen this gift in operation over the past two decades, and the consistency is remarkable. Always biblical, practical, applicable, and invariably served with a heaping side dish of warm-hearted humor. Thomas is relatable, and his genuine personal interest in others makes any time spent with him a joy.

As a consultant on a variety of issues and concerns, his wide experience in leadership enables him to deliver every time. This book will introduce you to the powerfully life-affirming encouragement that all who know this man are blessed!"

Myles Holmes
Lead Pastor
REVIVE
Maryville, Illinois
ReviveUSA.net

Factual Accounts of
Courage, Hope, and Inspiration
Told in Story, Song, and Scripture

MOVE UP!
DON'T GIVE UP!

THOMAS HARRISON

Foreword by **Roberta Roberts Potts**

dustjacket

Copyright ©2021 Thomas Harrison
Move Up! Don't Give Up!: Factual Accounts of Courage, Hope, and Inspiration Told in Story, Song, and Scripture / Thomas Harrison

Published by Dust Jacket Press
ISBN: 9-79-8515785-70-3

All rights reserved. No portion of this publication may be reproduced, stored in a retrieval system, or transmitted in any form or by any means, except in the case of brief quotations embodied in reviews or articles, without prior permission of Thomas Harrison. Contact the author: **ThomasMyFriend@aol.com**

While the author has made every effort to provide accurate internet addresses at the time of publication, neither the publisher nor the author assumes any responsibility for errors or for changes that occur after publication. Further, the publisher does not have any control over and does not assume any responsibility for author or third-party websites or their content.

Amplified Bible (AMP), Scripture quotations taken from the Amplified® Bible (AMP), Copyright © 2015 by The Lockman Foundation, Used by permission. www.Lockman.org

Common English Bible (CEB), Copyright © 2011 by Common English Bible. All rights reserved.

Complete Jewish Bible (CJB), Copyright © 1998 by David H. Stern. All rights reserved.

Contemporary English Version (CEV), Copyright © 1995 American Bible Society. All rights reserved.

English Standard Version (ESV), Scripture quotations are from The Holy Bible, English Standard Version® (ESV®), copyright © 2001 by Crossway, a publishing ministry of Good News Publishers. Used by permission. All rights reserved.

Good News Translation (GNT), Scripture quotations marked (GNT) are from the Good News Translation in Today's English Version- Second Edition Copyright © 1992 by American Bible Society. Used by Permission.

God's Word Translation (GWT), Scripture is taken from GOD'S WORD®, © 1995 God's Word to the Nations. Used by permission of Baker Publishing Group.

J.B. Phillips New Testament (Phillips), J. B. Phillips, "The New Testament in Modern English", 1962 edition, published by HarperCollins.

King James Version (KJV), Public Domain

New Century Version (NCV) The Holy Bible, New Century Version®. Copyright © 2005 by Thomas Nelson, Inc.

New International Version (NIV), THE HOLY BIBLE, NEW INTERNATIONAL VERSION®, NIV® Copyright © 1973, 1978, 1984, 2011 by Biblica, Inc.™ Used by permission. All rights reserved worldwide.

New Living Translation (NLT), Holy Bible, New Living Translation copyright © 1996, 2004, 2007 by Tyndale House Foundation. Used by permission of Tyndale House Publishers Inc., Carol Stream, IL 60188. All rights reserved. New Living, NLT, and the New Living Translation logo are registered trademarks of Tyndale House Publishers.

The Expanded Bible (TEB), Scripture taken from The Expanded Bible. Copyright ©2011 by Thomas Nelson. Used by permission. All rights reserved.

The Message (Message), Scripture taken from The Message. Copyright © 1993, 1994, 1995, 1996, 2000, 2001, 2002. Used by permission of NavPress Publishing Group.

Cover Design: Rick Wyers, Lithaprint.com
Interior design: D. E. West, ZAQ Designs & Dust Jacket Creative Services
Editor: Roberta Roberts Potts
Encouragement: Kathy Harrison
Photography: Christina Bullard, KC Photography; Muskogee, Oklahoma

Printed in the United States of America

www.dustjacket.com

DEDICATION

This book is dedicated to:

Kathy
A virtuous woman is a crown to her husband.
Psalm 12:4a (KJV)

My Family
Look at how good and pleasing it is when
families live together as one!
Psalm 133:1 (CEB)

My Friends
Spend time with the wise and you will become wise.
Psalm 13:20a (NCE)

CONTENTS

FOREWORD

Who doesn't love stories? Everyone loves stories. I've always found it interesting that Jesus Himself — with all His knowledge, with all his ability, with all His limitless power — could easily have gone around the earth expounding His brilliance about anything and everything, fascinating all within His purview. Instead, He chose to tell stories.

Though he has an earned Ph.D., my long-time friend, Thomas Harrison, has wisely taken his cue from our Lord. What's so great about stories? For one thing, they're easy to remember, especially the meaning. While erudite rhetoric seems to so often glance off the memory banks of our already over-taxed brains, simple stories stick with us. I'm not sure why. They just do.

What makes a story great? They have to grab our insides and remind us of what we need to know or of what we used to know but have foolishly allowed adulthood to remove. But where do good stories come from? To write such a story you must have a gift of observation so acute that nothing escapes your eagle eye and your spirit must pick up on the slightest nuance of what you're watching. I suppose that's the first thing which stunned me about Thomas Harrison's stories. For I could have been in all the same places where Thomas sat — yet been totally oblivious to all that he saw. No fair! Unfortunately, I'm just not all that observant. Oh well, while God simply did not choose to give me that gift, He did give it to my friend. Thomas just seems to have the ability to see a situation and read through it. This is a true blessing from God and I'm so grateful God's gift is being used not for human aggrandizement, but for the glory of God.

So as you read this wonderful book, may the Lord quicken in your heart exactly what *you* need to know and exactly what *you* need to learn in order to make it just a little bit easier for Jesus to accomplish in you what is pleasing in His sight.

Roberta Roberts Potts

P.S. My very favorite of all Thomas' stories was the one he calls "God is Ready to Scoop us Up." Oh my. It touched my heart so much I was ready to call an ambulance for the little boy before I gave myself an opportunity to even finish reading the story!

INTRODUCTION

The universe is made up of stories, not atoms.
Muriel Rukeyser

Stories bond each of us together in the human experience of life. Our ancestors knew the power of stories, both real and imagined. Such stories stirred the minds and passed along family history through oral tradition.

The interconnectedness of stories moves our emotions, kindles our passions, and enlists us to thought and action.

When the children of Israel crossed the Jordan River on dry ground with the Ark of the Lord's Covenant, God instructed them to take twelve stones to build a memorial of God's deliverance. The account is recorded in Joshua 4:1-7. They were to place twelve stones as a sign for when the "children ask their fathers in time to come, saying, what mean ye by these stones." God knew inquiring minds would ask at some point why the stones were assembled.

Pastors use illustrations to communicate the points of their sermons. Such examples are told and retold long after the sermons are forgotten.

In memorial services, we eulogize the deceased by sharing stories of their life struggle and victories.

Actors, poets, singers, philosophers, and artists use stories to bridge the gap between the concrete and abstract elements of life.

The New Testament books of Matthew and Mark record a near-identical verse which tells us Jesus taught in parables and told his followers the meaning of those parables.

*"All these things spake Jesus unto the multitude in
parables; and without a parable spake he not unto them."*
Matthew 13:34 (KJV).

*"But without a parable spake he not unto them:
and when they were alone, he expounded
all things to his disciples."*
Mark 4:34 (KJV).

Sharing the testimony of one's faith or deliverance is a practice of the church dating back to its origins at Pentecost. Compelling stories of struggle and victory encourage believers, seekers, and those without hope or faith.

The following pages are a collection of stories, illustrations, and observations that I hope will inspire and encourage you. How this collection of stories came to be is a fascinating story.

I married a church musician, and as a *civilian* (non-musical person), I have often accompanied my wife to church for pre-service rehearsals. On one of these Sunday mornings, I was taking my usual place in the balcony for Kathy to join me once the choir and orchestra completed their portion of the service. In short, I was saving a seat for my wife. After reading the church worship bulletin, there was still more waiting before the service began and the thought came to me to create a text message of encouragement for my pastor friends. Thus, in 2013 I started an almost every Sunday message to my network. A thought, scripture, hymn, or observation would come to mind, and I typed the text message on my iPhone. I would copy and paste the message, adding a personal salutation, including the recipient's first name.

When my personal and professional schedule increased my travel, I wrote the Sunday greetings in the back of a taxi, waiting in airport terminals, hotel rooms, and rest stops by the side of the road.

I would prefer to report that I knew from the beginning that the messages would one day become a book, but such would be untrue. It was just that Sunday by Sunday, year after year, I sent messages to encourage and bless my friends.

My pastor friends were kind with comments, and many would ask, "Could I use this in today's message or tonight's board meeting?" Some would repost on social media. Others would comment, "I needed to hear this."

One by one my friends encouraged me to compile the messages into a book to help others. Such were the humble beginnings of what you hold in your hand or are perusing on the screen of your computer device.

Move Up! Don't Give Up! is a collection of encouraging stories, songs, and scriptures to offer courage, hope, and inspiration. If this book brings smiles or tears, laughter or cheers, would you consider sharing that thought or this book with another?

Thomas Harrison
Tulsa, Oklahoma
February 1, 2021

The ability to do something which frightens one*

Strength in the face of pain or grief*

Mental or moral strength to persevere and
withstand danger, fear, or difficulty**

*Have not I commanded thee? Be strong and of a good courage;
be not afraid, neither be thou dismayed:
for the LORD thy God is with thee whithersoever thou goest.*
Joshua 1:9 (KJV)

---

*Courage | Definition of courage by Oxford dictionary on Lexico.com also meaning of courage. (n.d.). Lexico Dictionaries | English. https://www.lexico.com/en/definition/courage

**Definition of courage. (n.d.). Dictionary by Merriam-Webster: America's most-trusted online dictionary. https://www.merriam-webster.com/dictionary/courage

THE STRONGEST MAN
IN OUR NEIGHBORHOOD

My father was the strongest man in our neighborhood. He could have been one of those men on TV ripping to shreds thick telephone directories. Born ten days before the stock market crash of 1929, he made his living by repairing American-made cars for his employer and on the side in our garage behind our home. One day while working on the underbody of a car, its support and lift system collapsed right on top of him. The good news is that he was able to survive a life-threatening injury. But afterward, the doctor understandably encouraged my father to consider a different occupation! But since my dad had only attended school through the 8th grade, he and my mother were stumped. How in the world was my father to support our family now? The doctor suggested he work on cars which were not as heavy, but as it was in the early 1960s, the only lighter vehicles were foreign, and imported vehicles were unpopular then as World War II was so fresh in everyone's mind.

But having few alternatives, after his discharge from the hospital, my father began working almost exclusively on imported cars. He founded one of the few independent auto repair facilities specializing in imported vehicles. Then both an oil embargo, and rising gas prices changed everything! Imported cars became popular due to their styling and gas mileage. Attorneys, doctors, and insurance adjusters brought their cars to my father for repair. He moved his business from facility to facility to keep up with the high demand. Eventually, he custom-designed a repair facility. Dad had an eye for detail and his paint work was flawless. He began a wrecker service and sold used cars from a corner lot of the facility. Over the years he employed scores of people and my brother now operates the business Dad started.

My father had no way of knowing what the future held, but God knew. Only God knew of the coming oil embargo and rising gas prices. Only God knew that what had sustained our family thus far would soon be removed. Why didn't God keep my dad from having that terrible accident? I don't know, but I know that we live in a fallen world where Satan comes only to "steal and kill and destroy." John 10:10 (KJV) And I know this as well. When it seemed there was no way for him to continue supporting his family, my father had a choice. He could give up or he could move up. I thank God he didn't give up!

IN GREAT HARDSHIP BEAUTIFUL THINGS ARE BIRTHED

In times of great hardship beautiful things are birthed.

"The Father of Gospel" Thomas A. Dorsey lost his first wife as she gave birth to their son who died two days later. Grieving the loss of his wife and son, Dorsey wrote a song that brought him fame and fortune.

"Precious Lord,
take my hand
Lead me on, let me stand
I am tired, I'm weak, I am worn
Through the storm, through the night
Lead me on to the light
Take my hand, precious Lord
Lead me home."

Precious Lord
Thomas A. Dorsey
©1932

In distressing times God builds character and births beautiful things. We never know what legacy we are building now. Our greatest work may be just ahead.

Be encouraged today my friend. I believe in you!

Hymnary.org is my primary research website for lyrics, author biography, and history of sacred music.

WE'VE ALL BEEN THERE

"Great is my boldness of speech toward you,
great is my glorying of you: I am filled with comfort,
I am exceeding joyful in all our tribulation."
2 Corinthians 7:4 (KJV)

We've all been there. Unfounded accusations, insults, gossip, and mean-spiritedness have attacked from out of the blue.

We question our motives, thoughts, and actions. We are innocent: yet our accusers scream louder.

During such times it is important to remain calm and cheerful. These attacks sting; yet those around us are watching how we handle life.

As sure as the ancients accused Jesus; we will be accused.

We must hold our head high; apparently, we are doing something grand! Pray for our accusers. Correct what needs correcting and move forward.

We speak and act in boldness as we proclaim the goodness of God.

Hold on my friend, new supporters are coming your way.

SMILING AT OUR FOES

"Glorious things of thee are spoken,
Zion, city of our God!
He, whose Word cannot be broken,
Formed thee for His own abode.
On the Rock of Ages founded,
What can shake thy sure repose?
With salvation's walls surrounded,
Thou may'st smile at all thy foes."

Glorious Things of Thee are Spoken
Words: John Newton
Music: Franz J. Hayden
1799

I remind you of this old hymn from the 1700s which tells us how wonderful God is! Then it tells us how we were formed by God with assurance that our faith (repose) and salvation are sure. The last line is humorous as an inside joke -smiling at our foes!

Today may you go forth in power and anointing of the Holy Spirit: assured of your faith, salvation and calling. For those who may elect to oppose you-smile! Their efforts are futile. This hymn ends with this assurance:

"Solid joys and lasting treasure None but Zion's children know."

I am incredibly proud of you today. Go forth and enjoy the day God has given you!

Hymnary.org is my primary research website for lyrics, author biography, and history of sacred music.

YOUR RIGHTEOUSNESS WILL BE REWARDED

*"The Lord has brought about our vindication and has
revealed the righteousness of our cause; Come and let us
proclaim in Zion the work of the Lord our God!"*
Jeremiah 51:10 (AMP)

There will come a day when you will be vindicated. Your righteousness will be rewarded and truth shall be revealed.

I believe that time will occur in Heaven but also here on earth.

Whatever has been pressing against you—you will be vindicated.

When that day comes, revel in its sweetness as a gift from God.

Until then, be confident in the fact that righteousness is on your side. God is fighting for you!

JESUS PAID IT ALL

"I hear the Savior say,
"Thy strength indeed is small;
Child of weakness, watch and pray,
Find in Me thine all in all."

And when before the throne
I stand in Him complete,
I'll lay my trophies down,
All down at Jesus' feet."

Jesus Paid It All
Elvina Hall
1865

My friend, we may have more questions than answers. We may have more doubts than faith. We may have uncertainty in the face of challenges.

God freely provides for us answers, faith, and courage in great abundance. Listen for His voice. If He spoke to Moses, He'll speak to you. If He encouraged David at his lowest point, God will encourage you. If the Angel of the Lord called cowardly Gideon a mighty man of valor, God sees you that way also.

I am proud of you!

Hymnary.org is my primary research website for lyrics, author biography, and history of sacred music.

GOD MAKES ME WALK FORWARD WITH SPIRITUAL CONFIDENCE

*"The Lord God is my strength my source of courage,
my invincible army; He has made my feet steady
and sure like hinds' feet and makes me walk forward
with spiritual confidence on my high places
of challenge and responsibility."*
Habakkuk 3:19 (AMP)

May you move forward in spiritual confidence with strength as you accept the challenge and responsibility!

I believe in you!

MAKE NO LITTLE PLANS HERE

"Be brave. Be strong. Don't give up. Expect God to get here soon."
Psalm 31:24 (Message)

There is a great comfort knowing God is on the way! Even in good times, when things are going our way we often wonder if this is all God may have for us. My friend God is on your side. He wants you to excel. Begin to dream big dreams.

While building Oral Roberts University, Oral Roberts had a sign on his desk: "Make no little plans here." This reminded Oral--and everyone who came into his office--to dream BIG.

I have a replica of that sign in my office, reminding me to dream big.

My friend, write that saying on your heart and mind.

In your life, the life of the church, and your family–"Make no little plans here."

TWO OVERCOATS?

"If you have two coats, give one away," he said.
"Do the same with your food."
Luke 3:11 (Message)

During a nationwide cold weather weekend, my friend of more than 40 years suggested we have lunch with a friend of his. I agreed. While walking in the cold and bitter wind, I noticed two of us wearing overcoats, but my friend was wearing a windbreaker.

Later, I asked my friend if I could give him an old overcoat. He was elated as he had no winter coat, much less a dress winter coat. (Additionally, I gave him an extra scarf and a pair of dress leather gloves.) While the coat had sentimental value, I no longer wore it. My friend was cold and it moved me. My surplus became his abundance. I had always taken this verse figuratively until that week.

Friends, those around us can't see and hear our message of the Gospel if they are shivering trying to stay warm and are hungry.

I am thankful God opened my eyes and my heart to someone in need. I gave of my surplus and the need was met. I have been blessed in many ways, but nothing in recent memory has blessed me as much as knowing my surplus overcoat is keeping my friend warm.

GOD, I'VE HEARD WHAT
OUR ANCESTORS SAY ABOUT YOU

"God, I've heard what our ancestors say about you,
and I'm stopped in my tracks, down on my knees.
Do among us what you did among them.
Work among us as you worked among them.
And as you bring judgment,
as you surely must, remember mercy."
Habakkuk 3:1-2 (Message)

May Habakkuk's prayer be your prayer today.

THE BOMB SHELTER GIVES BIRTH

"Surrounded then as we are by these serried ranks
of witnesses, let us strip off everything that hinders us,
as well as the sin which dogs our feet, and let us run the race
that we have to run with patience, our eyes fixed on Jesus the
source and the goal of our faith. For he himself endured a cross and
thought nothing of its shame because of the joy he knew
would follow his suffering; and he is now seated at the right
hand of God's throne. Think constantly of him enduring
all that sinful men could say against him and
you will not lose your purpose or your courage."
Hebrews 12: 1-3 (Phillips)

During World War II, while a minister at Church of the Good Shepherd in London, John Bertram Phillips, (more famously known as J.B. Phillips) saw that the young people in his church had difficulty understanding the current version of the Bible. Additionally, he had his own problems, having suffered a near death experience while in his 20s and also being forced to deal with clinical depression throughout his life. Then came the now famous Battle for Britain which had to have been indescribably deafening for every individual Londoner.

Yet what Germany saw as a most horrific battle to capture England, Phillips saw as time which would have otherwise been wasted, a golden opportunity to start a modern translation of the King James Version of the Bible. While sitting in bomb shelters during the London Blitz, this minister began a translation of the New Testament into modern English, starting with the Epistle to the Colossians. The results appealed to the young people who found it easier to understand.

My friend, whatever you are facing, keep smiling. God is up to something in your life. What are you working on while in the bomb shelter? Ask God to show you what it is. Keep writing, keep singing, keep preaching, keep being creative even during the heat of the battle.

J.B. Phillips New Testament (Phillips) - Version information - BibleGateway.com. (n.d.). BibleGateway.com: A searchable online Bible in over 150 versions and 50 languages. https://www.biblegateway.com/versions/JB-Phillips-New-Testament/

John Bertram Phillips. (2006, March 29). Wikipedia, the free encyclopedia. Retrieved December 25, 2020, from https://en.wikipedia.org/wiki/John_Bertram_Phillips

"FEAR DOES NOT STOP DEATH; IT STOPS LIFE."

Jim McNabb

Pastor

The Bridge

wearethebridge.church

Used by permission.

MAY THE LORD ANSWER YOU IN THE DAY OF TROUBLE!

May the Lord answer you in the day of trouble!

May the name of the God of Jacob set you securely on high (and defend you in battle)!

May He send you help from the sanctuary (His dwelling place) and support and strengthen you from Zion!

May He remember all your meal offerings and accept your burnt offering. Selah.

May He grant you your heart's desire and fulfill all your plans.

We will sing joyously over your victory, and in the name of our God we will set up our banners.

May the Lord fulfill all your petitions.

Psalm 20: 1-5 (AMP)

GOD IS READY TO SCOOP US UP

"Thus saith the Lord God, Behold,
I will lift up mine hand to the Gentiles,
and set up my standard to the people:
and they shall bring thy sons in their arms,
and thy daughters shall be
carried upon their shoulders."
Isaiah 49:22 (KJV)

The beautiful Fairmont Scottsdale Princess was my home for three days as I worked for a corporate client during the 2014 Christmas season.

The hotel decorates everything with Christmas lights. Beautiful displays on the lagoon, a golf-cart train ride through the light displays, an outdoor skating rink, and Christmas carolers. It's quite the production! Families come by the scores to walk the paths and see the lights.

One night I watched ice skaters on the outdoor rink. What a beautiful sight! One little boy-older than a toddler and not yet in elementary school-was ice skating and holding on to the rail. Right in front of me he falls. Nothing remarkable. He doesn't cry, whimper or make a sound. He stays put. A few seconds later a very tall young man skates over to him and scoops his son off the ice. The dad sets the boy on his feet and sends him on his way. The father stays until the boy is making progress around the edge of the ice holding on to the rail.

How many times does our Father God come to scoop us up from our falls and failures? The loving Father is always there waiting to scoop us up and set us on His way. Our duty during a setback is to remain silent and wait for God to scoop us up!

The outdoor carolers singing religious and seasonal Christmas music were largely ignored by the throng, yet the troupe kept singing. I stopped to enjoy the music. One-by-one, others stopped to listen and enjoy the music. Soon a large crowd had gathered to hear these voices praise God. The troupe began to sing more songs and sounded even better as more stopped to listen. That taught me when we see something beautiful or noble, we should stop, enjoy, and support.

God is speaking everywhere and all the time. We must make time to stop and enjoy the lesson God provides for us.

I am incredibly proud of you. Be encouraged today, knowing that no matter what happens God is ready to scoop you up in His arms and set you on the right path.

Love and bless the people today-especially those who have no one to encourage them!

PARALYZED BY FEAR?

"Be strong. Take courage. Don't be intimidated.
Don't give them a second thought because God your
God is striding ahead of you. He's right there with you.
He won't let you down; he won't leave you."
Deuteronomy 31:6 (Message)

God's favor is on you today and every day. Be strong and use the courage God gives you to explore new areas, try new things, bring peace and prosperity to your household. There are battles and opposition, most certainly.

Years ago, in the heat of fierce opposition and personal attack, I was paralyzed with fear. My spiritual father Rev. Ossie Jones told me "I pity the people who oppose you! They really don't know what they are doing!"

I was floored at his response. However, in that situation and many others, God protected me and blessed me. I now see each battle with fresh eyes of faith.

My friend, God's favor is on you today. Take courage.

PRAYING FOR ICE CREAM?

"Let us walk honestly, as in the day; not in rioting and drunkenness, not in chambering and wantonness, not in strife and envying."
Romans 13:13 (KJV)

I read a news item about a group of pastors and believers who gathered to pray for the Blue Bell Ice Cream company.

An outbreak of listeria had occurred at several Blue Bell production facilities. Despite the company's cleaning efforts, the outbreak could not be contained and unfortunately caused death and illness. Ice cream products had been recalled and the plants closed.

I thought this prayer meeting was beautiful and fitting. People gathered to pray, wanting to peaceably and quietly support the company. Others in our nation take a different route causing rioting, protests, and lawsuits.

We are to be ministers of peace and reconciliation. Let us set the example in our home, church, communities, and nation.

I am very proud of you today!

After recall, town rallies around ice cream company. (2015, April 26). al. https://www.al.com/news/index.ssf/2015/04/prayers_for_blue_bell_after_re.html

PRAYING FOR OTHERS

*"After Job had prayed for his friends, the Lord restored his fortunes
and gave him twice as much as he had before."*
Job 42:10 (NIV)

Friend, this verse is a key to our success. I have always believed if we take care of God's business, He will take care of our business.

When we need a breakthrough, an answer or a physical need met — pray for your friends. The secret of happiness, and prosperity is in blessing others.

Find someone and make them your prayer project. Don't tell them, just pray. Watch God move as your friend is blessed.

Praise God as the answers come and your needs are met.

I am incredibly proud of you today. May you be blessed many times over in every area of your life.

YOUR LAST FRIEND IS MORE POWERFUL THAN YOUR LAST DOLLAR

*"Just as iron sharpens iron, friends sharpen
the minds of each other."*
Proverbs 27:17 (CEV)

*"Just as iron sharpens iron, a person sharpens the
character of his friend."*
Proverbs 27:17 (CJB)

"As iron sharpens iron, so people can improve each other."
Proverbs 27:17 (EB)

*"As iron sharpens iron, so one person
sharpens the wits of another."*
Proverbs 27:17 (GWT)

If you have spent any time with me, you know friendship is a character trait I honor. My friend Ed says: "Your last friend is more powerful than your last dollar!"

During one of our conversations, Ed related this story:

My friend's mentor had finished his first book; back in those simpler days of typewriters. With this book he had prepared 300 hand-drawn illustrations. Months of labor went into this how-to book. The man shipped it though UPS to the publisher but the manuscript never arrived!

The distraught man mentioned this to his friend and the friend said: "I give you permission to find the power to redo this." The man worked and produced a second version which was shipped to the publisher. The second version was actually better than the first. This book became a staple in the industry and thousands have enjoy- ed the second and better version.

It is often stated that Winston Churchill failed the 6th grade. Later in life when asked about failing in school, Churchill replied that he had never failed. He said he was only given a second opportunity to succeed.

My friend, I believe in you! God and I are on your side! If you have failed, or you are not sure you have done your best, the word I have for you today is: "I give you permission to find the power to redo this!" You have a second opportunity to succeed.

Desire accompanied by expectation
of or belief in fulfillment*

*"Therefore my heart is glad, and my glory rejoiceth:
my flesh also shall rest in hope."*
Psalm 16:9 (KJV)

*Definition of hope. (n.d.). Dictionary by Merriam-Webster: America's most-trusted online dictionary. https://www.merriam-webster.com/dictionary/hope

FEELING LIKE AN UNDERDOG?

As a child I watched Saturday morning cartoons and one of my favorites was Underdog. It was silly, but it helped me and my friends understand that sometimes the underdog becomes the hero. There is something about an underdog which attracts us. Perhaps it is because we want the little guy to win. Or maybe it's because we see ourselves as an underdog trying to overcome.

In the midst of a perfectly dreadful day and very long night, God reminded me of others who had fallen on rough times. Daniel, a faithful servant of God faced the company of lions. (Daniel 6) What about the boy and his widowed mother facing starvation in a time of famine in the land? (1 Kings 17) What about all those prophets Obadiah hid in caves because Jezebel was trying to kill them? (1 Kings 18:4)

God loves underdogs too. There are times in our lives when we are the least, the untouchable, the outcast, and the one who is not good enough.

Sometimes our cry to the Lord is "Look at me and help me! I'm all alone and in big trouble." Psalm 25:16 (Message)

My friend, I know you face such days too! Let us both be encouraged by this verse:

"God, my God, I yelled for help and you put me together. God, you pulled me out of the grave, gave me another chance at life when I was down-and-out." Psalm 30: 2-3 (Message)

My friend, I am very proud of you! I know we face challenges in life. Sometimes those challenges seem more than we can handle. Rest assured; God is helping YOU! God will bring YOU out, through and over!

FRIEND, MOVE UP!

"Friend...move up to a better place..."
Luke 14:10 (NIV)

This passage tells us the importance of taking a lesser seat at a gathering and the host inviting us to move up.

This scripture reminds me of the duty we have toward our friends. We should constantly tell them, "friend, move up."

Move up to a better way of thinking. Move up in better ways of behavior. Move up in our lifestyle. We should continuously be on the move up!

My friend, I hope to always encourage you with my words and actions.

Move up, my friend.

I am incredibly proud of you and for our friendship.

"For all those words which were written long ago
are meant to teach us today; that when we read in
he scriptures of the endurance of men and of all the
help that God gave them in those days, we may be
encouraged to go on hoping in our own time."
Romans 15:4 (Phillips)

May we all be encouraged to continue to hope!

(This message was written in 2013 and was among the first Sunday greetings I sent to my network via text message.)

IF YOU CARE, YOU WILL PREPARE

"If you care, you will prepare."
Dr. Thomas Harrison

I have used this phrase for more than 25 years while training leaders and advising those in ministry, business, non-profit, media, and educational organizations.

Prepare is a verb (an action word) meaning the process of making something (or someone) ready and available for a future time or event.

My grandfather would preserve, or *save* (as the country folk called it) fruits and produce by canning them in glass jars and storing them in the cellar on his northwest Arkansas farm.

I hated going to the cellar due to the coldness, darkness and bugs. However, I loved the product which came from the process. Fruit, corn, potatoes, tomatoes, green beans, and snap peas provided for our enjoyment in winter or when the crops were not bountiful.

When God saves his children, He prepares them for a future use. He cares for us, and thus prepares us.

Whatever we are experiencing, whatever we have done, we know this: God is preparing us for His future use.

I AM READY TO GO

"Blessed be God, the God-of-Our-Fathers,
who put it in the mind of the king to beautify The Temple
of God in Jerusalem! Not only that, he caused the king and all
his advisors and influential officials actually to like me and
back me. My God was on my side and I was ready to go.
And I organized all the leaders of Israel to go with me."
Ezra 7:27, 28 (Message)

This verse should energize us:

1. God will send important people to us to help His work.

2. God will send us to important people to help us.

3. We will be "liked" and have favor with those we meet.

4. We will lead "like-minded" people to be our friends, and associates.

5. The necessary finances will be provided.

My friend, let us be like Ezra and say "I AM ready to go!"

WHATEVER (SEEMINGLY) LIES DORMANT

"Abraham, when hope was dead within him,
went on hoping in faith, believing that he would become
"the father of many nations". He relied on the word of God
which definitely referred to 'your descendants.'"
Romans 4:18 (Phillips)

May whatever (seemingly) lies dormant and dead within your life, family, work, and ministry spring to life and bring blessings to the current and future generations.

THIS IS NOT THE END OF YOUR STORY

"With undaunted faith he looked at the facts—
his own impotence (he was practically a hundred years
old at the time) and his wife Sarah's apparent barrenness.
Yet he refused to allow any distrust of a definite pronouncement of
God to make him waver. He drew strength from his faith, and while
giving the glory to God, remained absolutely convinced that
God was able to implement his own promise. This was the "faith"
which 'was accounted to him for righteousness.'"
Romans 4:19 (Phillips)

My friend, we are not too old to see The Promise come to be in our lives. Whatever your promise—hold on—don't quit.

Wherever you are today—this is not the end of your story.

Let us hold on to God's faith in us while we hold on to our faith in God.

God bless you my friend.

I am exceptionally proud of you!

THE STEADFAST LOVE OF THE LORD

"The steadfast love of the Lord never ceases;
His mercies never come to an end;
They are new every morning;
Great is your faithfulness."
Lamentations 3 :22-23 (ESV)

A footnote to verse 22 indicates that in the original Hebrew, the verse is rendered: Because of the steadfast love of the Lord, we are not cut off.

These verses were made popular by Edith McNeil in her song *The Steadfast Love of the Lord.*

May we find the reality of verse 22 in the original Hebrew: Because of the love of God, we will not be cut off! My friend, whatever you are facing, know God loves you and has the best prepared for you—YOU will not be cut off!

Hymnary.org is my primary research website for lyrics, author biography, and history of sacred music.

A SHELTER IN THE TIME OF STORM

"The Lord's our Rock, in Him we hide,
A shelter in the time of storm;
Secure whatever ill betide
A Shelter in the time of storm.

Refrain
Oh, Jesus is a Rock in a weary land,
A weary land, a weary land;
Oh, Jesus is a Rock in a weary land,
A shelter in the time of storm."

A Shelter in the Time of Storm
Vernon J. Charlesworth
(*circa 1880*)

Some days after an hour or so of grappling with the storms of life, you feel like crawling back in bed with your pillow jammed down over your head as tight as you can stand it. Maybe it's hearing the news, maybe it's just hearing the baby cry... again. Or maybe it's the boss expecting things from you that you simply cannot deliver. Sometimes we simply want to hide out from anything and everybody.

But that's the time the words of old hymns such as this can bring solace and encouragement. While in such moments the world all too often simply looks for the nearest bar, in our God we find a Rock.

May you find comfort and strength in God's power, protection, and direction.

I have an overflowing appreciation of you today!

Hymnary.org is my primary research website for lyrics, author biography, and history of sacred music.

JUST AS I AM

"Just as I am - though toss'd about
With many a conflict, many a doubt,
Fightings and fears within, without,
-O Lamb of God, I come!"

Just As I Am
Charlotte Elliott
(1835)

"We, therefore, can confidently say:
'The Lord is my helper; I will not fear.
What can man do to me?'"
Hebrews 13:6 (Phillips)

May God comfort all your fears, within and without.

Hymnary.org is my primary research website for lyrics, author biography, and history of sacred music.

I WOKE UP WITH HEAVEN ON MY MIND

One Sunday morning, I awoke with these lyrics running through my mind:

"I woke up this morning feeling fine,
I woke up with heaven on my mind
…I'm feeling fine…"

I'm Feeling Fine
Mosie Lister

This song reminds me that how I feel is a choice. Aches and pains might try to hinder us, but our mind is our biggest hindrance.

Let us determine to keep heaven on our mind and always keep our minds feeling fine with a great attitude.

Personalize this verse:

"Let (your name in the possessive) light so shine before men,
that they may see (your name in the possessive)
good works and glorify (your name in the possessive)
Father which is in heaven."
Matthew 5:16 (KJV)

Hymnary.org is my primary research website for lyrics, author biography, and history of sacred music.

SOMETHING NEW IS ON ITS WAY

*"Forget about what's happened; don't keep
going over old history. Be alert, be present. I'm about to
do something brand-new. It's bursting out! Don't you see it?
There it is! I'm making a road through the desert, rivers in the
badlands. Wild animals will say 'Thank you!' —the coyotes and the
buzzards— Because I provided water in the desert, rivers through
the sun-baked earth, Drinking water for the people I chose,
the people I made especially for myself, a people
custom-made to praise me."*
Isaiah 43: 18-21 (Message)

COMFORT FOR THE JOURNEY

*"In the multitude of my thoughts within me
thy comforts delight my soul."*
Psalm 94:19 (KJV)

Often, we run on empty, rushing from one event to the next. Our love for God's people compels us to continue but without regular visits at the "service station," it won't be long before we'll be like those old clunkers we often view sitting beside the expressway—abandoned and waiting for a tow truck. Like those vehicles, when we run on empty — no time to commune with the Holy Spirit, no time to commune with other believers, no time to spend on our knees — well, let's just say we truly need the comforts the Psalmist was describing!

Today may the God of all comfort encourage your heart and spirit.

May you spend the requisite time with the Comforter, reading and studying His Word, blessing His holy name and "tuning up" all that is within you. As you do so, may your body be renewed so that you may be able to continue to labor in the vineyard with renewed energy and focus.

While I so wish I could be with you today, to help shadow and encourage you, how amazing it is to know that wherever you are, our mighty God surrounds you. He is your refuge, your fortress and your exceeding joy! I am most thankful for the unique role you serve in the body of Christ.

Find comfort for the journey and in that your soul will delight.

WHEN WE SEEK GOD, HE REWARDS US

"But without faith it is impossible to please him:
for he that cometh to God must believe that he is, and that he
is a rewarder of them that diligently seek him."
Hebrews 11:6 (KJV)

This is my life verse.

When we seek God, He rewards us.

As we build looking forward to living the dream, we must trust God in the build stage as much as we bless Him in the dream stage.

While we build and live our dream; let us help others build *their* dream!

Trust the Lord of the Build *and* the Lord of the Dream.

Build and Live the Dream.

I am wholeheartedly and unreservedly proud of you!

TRUST YOUR GUIDE

"Thou will shew me the path of life: in thy presence is fullness of joy;
at thy right hand there are pleasures for evermore."
Psalm 16:11 (KJV)

"Every road I've travelled down, you have walked before me"

The King of Who I Am
Tanya Goodman & Michael Sykes
(C) 1983

No matter which road we travel—God has been there before us. His sustaining grace and presence in our life assures us He knows the way. We can follow His direction with complete confidence.

Wherever your journeys are taking you during this season of life—rejoice—God is taking good care of you! He knows the path—trust your guide.

Hymnary.org is my primary research website for lyrics, author biography, and history of sacred music.

ALL MY HOPE IS IN JESUS

"All my hope is in Jesus
Thank God my yesterday's gone.
All my sins are forgiven
I've been washed by the blood."

All My Hope*
David Crowder
Ed Cash
(C) 2016

How often does our own concept of ourselves keep us from being the best we can be, the best of ourselves and more importantly, the man or the woman God created us to be? We hear the words play over and over in our heads: "You're not good enough! You're not worthy!" And yes, that's right. We aren't worthy, but Jesus is! Jesus IS good enough. Jesus IS worthy. Yes, in ourselves we have no hope. Our hope, our only hope is in Jesus and what He thinks of us. And He must think a lot of you... or He would never have died for you.

May you be set free from anything which holds you back, in Jesus' name. Amen

Hymnary.org is my primary research website for lyrics, author biography, and history of sacred music.

---

*©2016 Inot Music (Admin. by Capitol CMG Publishing), sixsteps Music (Admin. by Capitol CMG Publishing), worshiptogether.com songs (Admin. by Capitol CMG Publishing), Alletrop Music (Admin. by Music Services, Inc.)

WHO CAN CHEER THE HEART LIKE JESUS?

"Who can cheer the heart like Jesus
By His presence all divine
True and tender, pure and precious
O, how blest to call Him mine

All that thrills my soul is Jesus
He is more than life to me
And the fairest of ten thousand
In my blessed Lord I see."

All That Thrills My Soul Is Jesus
Words and Music by
Thoro Harris
(C) 1931

Hymnary.org is my primary research website for lyrics, author biography, and history of sacred music.

"BE KINDER THAN NECESSARY!"

David Ingles
Songwriter, Founder: Oasis Radio Network
OasisNetwork.org
Used by permission.

TAKE 5 AND PREPARE FOR THE NEW YEAR!

A good habit to start each New Year is to make a list of the following:

> 5 accomplishments of the past year (Your achievements)
>
> 5 people you will help in the New Year (Your investment in others)
>
> 5 things you will accomplish in the New Year (Your goals)
>
> 5 people you will need to assist you in accomplishing your goals for the New Year (Resources or contacts you will need)
>
> 5 things you will improve or learn in the New Year (Your personal development plan)

Become a better you. Give more. Learn more. Develop more skills.

> *"And the* Lord *answered me, and said,*
> *Write the vision, and make it plain upon tables,*
> *that he may run that readeth it."*
> Habakkuk 2:2 (KJV)

I believe in you!

DON'T CURSE YOURSELF

"This day I call the heavens and the earth as
witnesses against you that I have set before you life and death,
blessings and curses. Now choose life, so that you and your
children may live and that you may love the Lord your God,
listen to his voice, and hold fast to him. For the Lord is your life,
and he will give you many years in the land he swore to give
to your fathers, Abraham, Isaac and Jacob."
Deuteronomy 30:19-20 (NIV)

As I have traveled the United States and 5 countries, I continue to be amazed at the things people say. They speak of illness, disease, poverty, and lack. Sometimes these are spoken about their own life or the lives of their children or family. Why would we speak curses on ourselves and our family?

God desires us to speak good in all situations to everyone. Last week I told a friend "I am proud of you!" Later I received a reply that the words I spoke brought encouragement.

The old nursery rhyme: "Sticks and stones will break my bones; but words will never hurt me" is a lie. We often remember painful words long after the physical wound has healed.

Choose life! Speak life-affirming words to ourselves and those around us. God tells us that in doing so we and our children will be blessed and we will have a long and fruitful life and ministry.

Sometimes those words are faith statements as we act like God and speak those things that are not -- as though they were. (Romans 4:17)

We can change our words more quickly than we can change our behavior. So be patient with yourself and others today.

Whatever you are doing today, choose to speak life-affirming words.

I honor and bless you today in the name of Jesus!

20 MINUTES OF FAME
OR A LIFETIME OF SERVICE?

"Ye shall not need to fight in this battle: set yourselves,
stand ye still, and see the salvation of the LORD with you,
O Judah and Jerusalem: fear not, nor be dismayed; tomorrow
go out against them: for the LORD will be with you."
2 Chronicles 20:17 (KJV)

I was moved by Queen Elizabeth II's April 6, 2020 message to her nation as she encouraged citizens to be strong and stand firm as they fight against the virus.

Queen Elizabeth is the longest reigning monarch in history; 69 years on February 6, 2021. An impressive record for someone who will soon be 94 years old.

The briefest reign of any sovereign was Louis-Antoine of France, who in 1830 reigned for 20 minutes.

Queen Elizabeth has ruled for more than 36 million minutes (as of February 6, 2021). In terms of resoluteness, Queen Elizabeth's record is untouchable. Whether or not you agree with her politics, she is a formidable presence in the UK and the world.

Queen Elizabeth has outlived many of her detractors. Quietly, yet resolutely, she oversees more than 138 million people. Like many, she has trouble with her children and grandchildren.

There is much to be said for taking a stand, to continue day in and day out. One day becomes one month, one month becomes one year, one year becomes ten years. Soon a lifetime comes and vanishes.

Whatever our field, position, or ministry; we can learn much from Queen Elizabeth. Outlive your detractors. Don't be concerned about those who may have their 20 minutes of fame. Live your life by marching to the tune God gave you. Have good manners. Be known as a person of charity and benevolence. Encourage the troops who report to you. Honor those who serve above and beyond the call of duty.

Times such as these require resolute steadfastness. I believe you have those qualities.

Coronavirus: The Queen's message seen by 24 million. (2020, April 6). BBC News. https://www.bbc.com/news/entertainment-arts-52183327

Louis Antoine, Duke of Angoulême. (2004, December 3). Wikipedia, the free encyclopedia. Retrieved December 27, 2020, from https://en.wikipedia.org/wiki/Louis_Antoine,_Duke_of_Angoul%C3%AAme

THEY WITHOUT US SHOULD NOT BE MADE PERFECT

"And these all, having obtained a good report through faith, received not the promise: God having provided some better thing for us, that they without us should not be made perfect."
Hebrews 11:39-40 (KJV)

I believe everyone enjoys reading Hebrews 11, the Hall of Fame of Faith and Who's Who of the Patriarchs.

I have often wondered when our time has ended if those we leave behind will say we had accomplished great things for God. Notice the final two verses of this chapter. No matter how great these people were, they had not received the better way of Jesus. Should we think ourselves as insignificant, the concluding verse tells us "they without us should not be made perfect."

In the Kingdom—we need the patriarchs and modern saints for God's plan to be complete.

Yes, the patriarchs could have their sins covered, but Jesus' blood washes them away forever! Yes, the patriarchs had individual manifestations of the Holy Spirit from time to time, but we have the Holy Spirit dwelling within us! Let's stand in faith ready for what comes our way!

OUR PRESENCE SPEAKS VOLUMES

My major task a few years ago was to serve my family in support as my great nephew, Ezra, was dedicated to the Lord. I had no official function; however, my presence (or absence) speaks volumes.

My presence is a symbol of family unity; strength in numbers.

My presence endorses the ceremony, and I lend my approval by attending. I bestow my *imprimatur*.

My presence conveys I am active and involved with my family and what matters to them.

Our presence speaks volumes to those who watch us.

As leaders and organizers, our physical presence endorses and supports the activities and people involved.

Our presence builds confidence in those who lack courage.

Our presence is a beacon of strength and direction as people navigate uncertain paths.

Fellow laborer, make certain your physical presence endorses good and godly endeavors.

I am exuberantly proud of you!

(Photo by the author)

**The author and one of his great-nephews—Ezra.
One day Ezra will tell the story of his miraculous
arrival and survival. I can't wait!**

INSPIRATION

A divine influence directly and immediately
exerted upon the mind or soul.*

*"I alone know the plans I have for you,
plans to bring you prosperity and not disaster,
plans to bring about the future you hope for."*
Jeremiah 29:11 (GNT)

---

*Inspiration. (n.d.). www.dictionary.com. https://www.dictionary.com/browse/inspiration

HELP FROM AN OPPOSING PLAYER

I saw a television sports program which highlighted a basketball player with Down Syndrome. I watched him make a shot of a lifetime, thanks to a member of the opposing team.

How often we see ourselves as the weakest member of the team. Yet God uses our very weakness to demonstrate His strength in our lives. When we are frightened, confused, and vulnerable, God in His inimitable way seems to push us into action telling us to *suit up*.

> *"But quite the contrary, the parts of the body*
> *that seem to be weaker are [absolutely] necessary;*
> *and as for those parts of the body which we consider*
> *less honorable, these we treat with greater honor;*
> *and our less presentable parts are treated with greater*
> *modesty, while our more presentable parts*
> *do not require it. But God has combined the [whole] body,*
> *giving greater honor to that part which lacks it,*
> *so that there would be no division or discord in the body*
> *[that is, lack of adaptation of the parts to each other],*
> *but that the parts may have the same concern for one another.*
> *And if one member suffers, all the parts share the suffering;*
> *if one member is honored, all rejoice with it."*
> 1 Corinthians 12: 22-26 (AMP)

You are incredibly important to the Kingdom of God. Be encouraged. Be ready.

You can see the shot and read the story by following this link:
ABC News. (2016, March 15). Basketball team helps opposing player with Down syndrome score 'Epic shot'. Retrieved from https://abcnews.go.com/US/basketball-team-helps-opposing-player-syndrome-score-epic/story?id=37665642

WHAT'S IN YOUR HAND?

"Then the Lord said to him, What is that in your hand?
'A staff,' he replied."
Exodus 4:2 (NIV)

During a Palm Sunday service, the thought occurred to me how our palms (hands) can bless or hurt. God asked Moses "What's in your hand?" God used the very item in the hand of Moses to demonstrate His love and power.

I ask you today: "What's in your hand, friend?" Whatever God has placed in your hand--today and every day—it is there to show you God's love, His power, His deliverance and His blessing.

Use what you have been given today. It will bless you and others.

I continue to be proud of you. I am pleased with your success!

CELEBRATE OTHERS

"Let your light so shine before men that they
may see your moral excellence and your praiseworthy,
noble, and good deeds and recognize and honor and praise
and glorify your Father Who is in heaven."
Matthew 5:16 (AMP)

One weekend my wife and I traveled more than 800 miles to attend a wedding. A favorite pastime when I travel is to visit museums. I also enjoy visiting Presidential museums. We visited the Harry Truman and Dwight Eisenhower Presidential museums on the same day! Despite their politics, I believe we can learn much from each one who has held office as the President of the United States.

What impressed me in each of the two presidential museums I have also visited (Hoover and Lincoln) is how they served the people and how the people were empowered by their leader. Leaders understand the power of their authority. While these men were undoubtedly politicians, they were also true statesmen, holding their offices not merely to be re-elected but also to serve others.

While there is certainly scriptural precedent in giving and serving in secret, there are times when giving and serving should be done openly, for people need to see us investing in and serving others.

In his will, Basketball Hall of Fame coach Dean Smith provided $200 for each of the lettermen he coached during 36 seasons at the University of North Carolina at Chapel Hill. In celebrating others, we show our approval and investment in their accomplishments and lives.

Today I celebrate you and your accomplishments in life!

Rovell, D. (2015, March 26). Final gift: UNC's Smith leaves $200 to players. ESPN.com. https://www.espn.com/mens-college-basketball/story/_/id/12563125/former-north-carolina-tar-heels-coach-dean-smith-leaves-200-letterman

MINISTRY OF MAILING MEANINGFUL MESSAGES

*"Hearing of thy love and faith, which thou hast toward
the Lord Jesus, and toward all saints; That the communication
of thy faith may become effectual by the acknowledging of
every good thing which is in you in Christ Jesus."*
Philemon 1:5-6 (KJV)

Communication is critical in relationships, business transactions, and with family members.

While technology has presented us with multiple avenues for communication with others, at the same time it can become a slippery slope, a slope leading to hurt feelings as well as huge misunderstandings which were totally unnecessary from the start.

This week I noticed several *failure to communicate* moments. All could have been avoided.

When we become silos, in other words living in basic isolation, we (perhaps unintentionally) are thinking only of ourselves. Communication breaks the silence and brings life to relationships and other transactions of life. This week I was aware of a major situation a minister faced which could have been avoided simply by sending a thank you note.

Let me encourage you to become an Ambassador of Communication. Unlock the power of handwritten thank you notes. Resist the temptation to send an email or text as a thank you. While easy and time saving, such can come across as cold and little more than obligatory.

Send handwritten notes on birthday cards to family, and friends. Find ways to bring personal messages to others. Keep stacks of personalized note cards in your briefcase, car, office, and home. Purchase postage stamps and printed return address labels.

Prepare yourself for the ministry of sending meaningful messages in the mail. If you don't have one, invest in a quality roller ball pen or fountain pen. (Parker is my favorite but there are dozens on the market.). Keep refills on hand so you never lack having a supply of ink.

Yes, we must keep up with the times. Modern conveniences are wonderful in some ways, for example, when it means you can easily read and study the Bible on an airplane without having to lug a cumbersome King James around as was formerly necessary. The problem with modern conveniences though, is that sometimes they can come across as impersonal and therefore worse than useless. And because personal, handwritten thank you notes are now in the 21st century so refreshingly out of the ordinary, the response to what only took you a few minutes to write may surprise you. Remember, people are not used to receiving such things these days and it may just touch their hearts. I once received a thank you note for having sent a thank you note. Imagine that!

My friend, I care deeply about you and wish you to be a success in life. I hope this practical message has been helpful.

The author at his dining room table in Broken Arrow, Oklahoma writing thank you notes. (Photo by Kathy Harrison. Circa 1989)

WHO WOULD KNOW?

While I was Director of Communications for a large church near Tulsa, Oklahoma, my assignment was to create a video presentation for a fundraising banquet. Our goal was to create a video that told the history of the church and the opportunities which would come with a building at a new location.

My love for the church we attended for more than eighteen years, and my background in management of radio and television stations made this a dream assignment. I gathered materials (photographs, radio program recordings, letters, founding documents) to include in the video.

To provide the musical background, I selected several songs, including *Seventy Years Ago* by Twyla Paris and *For Such a Time as This* by Wayne Watson. We needed to secure rights to use these and other songs in the limited use video.

Having worked in broadcasting most of my life, I understood the system whereby artists and composers receive compensation for the use of their music. I contacted the music publishers with a healthy amount of concern as to whether the rights could be obtained and if the licensing fees would be affordable within our limited budget.

The first contract arrived in the mail, and I could not believe my eyes when I read the rights would cost $25. Indeed, this was an error. I called the publisher and asked if there had been a mistake in the calculation or perhaps in my communication of our project. The publisher's agent indicated the amount was correct and stated, "We only want churches to ask to use our music."

Asking to use something which does not belong to us seems old-fashioned by today's standards.

Indeed, there are those who use music, video, and other creative works without a second thought about securing permission. How would anyone know? It's all for God's kingdom, right?

Several years earlier, I heard a minister tell the story of his humble beginnings when he traveled from church to church singing and preaching. Offerings and sales of his music were meager and never seemed to adequately provide for his young family. He ministered at one church; as he was seated at the piano noticed a photocopied sheet music of a song he had written. His heart sank. He had come to minister to a church that had appropriated his music.

While the heart of man may convince us that our actions will never be discovered, we know God sees everything and knows the heart of man. "The eyes of the Lord are in every place, keeping watch on the evil and the good." Proverbs 15:3 (ESV) I could have used the music without permission or payment; who would have known? How could I knowingly steal from the artists and their representatives and then use the product to ask people to financially support a project for the church?

Total costs for the music rights for the fundraising video was slightly more than $100—a small price to retain the integrity of the project.

Victories were celebrated as the fundraising banquet exceeded all expectations and projections. God's people were enthusiastically generous. God always blesses us and others when we do what is right. God's eighth commandment is clear "Thou shalt not steal". Exodus 20:15 (KJV)

Comments on the video were overwhelmingly positive. I entered the video in a competition and received a Telly® Award for the project.

God blessed all who were involved in the project.

A PRISON OF OUR OWN MAKING

When I was General Manager of a Television Station in Tulsa, Oklahoma I hosted a weekly program, and this story was one I shared often.

Thomas Costain's History of England, *The Three Edwards*, described the life of Raynald III, the morbidly obese fourteenth century duke in what is now Belgium.

"After a violent quarrel, Raynald's younger brother
Edward led a successful revolt against him. Edward captured
Raynald but did not kill him. Instead, he built a room around
Raynald in Nieuwkerk castle and promised he could regain his title
and property as soon as he was able to leave the room."

"This would not have been difficult for most people
since the room had several windows and a door of
near-normal size, and none was locked or barred. The
problem was Raynald's size. To regain his freedom, he needed
to lose weight. But Edward knew his older brother, and each day
he sent a variety of delicious foods. Instead of dieting his way
out of prison, Raynald grew fatter. When Duke Edward was
accused of cruelty, he had a ready answer: "My brother is not
a prisoner. He may leave when he so wills." Raynald stayed
in that room for ten years and wasn't released until after
Edward died in battle. By then his health was so ruined he died
within a year, a prisoner of his own appetite."
–C.B. Larson (1999)

Many times, we are the prisoner of our own making. Something doesn't go as planned or we stumble and we place ourselves in a *prison* with no escape. Let us heed the words of Edward "He may leave when he so wills." Let's forgive ourselves, and let ourselves out of the prison we have made only for ourselves.

We are free in Christ Jesus today to be more than we are. Unless you are called to be a prison minister, life is better on the outside.

Larson, C. B. (1999). *Illustrations for preaching and teaching: From Leadership Journal.* Baker Publishing Group. Page 214

"I WOULD RATHER BE REMEMBERED FOR MY VICTORIES THAN FOR THE ABILITY TO RECALL IN INTRICATE DETAIL EVERY INJUSTICE."

Dr. Thomas Harrison

HALLELUJAH!

George Frideric Handel wrote the magnificent *Messiah* in 1741. The following year Handel was nearly destitute, yet convinced soloists and musicians to perform a benefit concert to debut the work. Ticket revenue was sufficient to pay the debts and release more than 150 men from debtor's prison.

The story doesn't end there.

Messiah was well received and to this day has brought the scriptures and God's love to millions. Incidentally the Messiah quotes from 81 Bible verses taken from 14 different books of the Bible (Jubal's Lyre, n.d.).

Handel found favor in Ireland where generous benefactors paid his debts. He continued to receive financial rewards for his works until his death. Handel bequeathed his fortune to a relative and a servant who remained with him for years.

A godly example of using one's gifts to help others while trusting God to bless you.

May this message bless you and spark within you financial and temporal blessings as you work on God's behalf.

Hymnary.org is my primary research website for lyrics, author biography, and history of sacred music.

George Frideric Handel. (2001, November 14). Wikipedia, the free encyclopedia. Retrieved December 20, 2020, from https://en.wikipedia.org/wiki/George_Frideric_Handel

Jubal's Lyre | Join the Eternal Song (n.d.). https://jubalslyre.com/wp-content/uploads/2015/12/Text-Study-of-Handels-Messiah.pdf
Messiah (Handel). (2020, December 6). Wikipedia, the free encyclopedia. Retrieved December 20, 2020, from https://en.wikipedia.org/wiki/Messiah_(Handel)

10 FEET TALL HOSPITAL VISIT

When I was a teenager, I often spent a week or so during the summer with my grandfather on his farm in Northwest Arkansas. He was a simple man but very wise. He never had much money, but he loved people and they loved him.

He explained that whenever he was feeling low, he would get dressed up and go into town to visit nursing homes and hospitals. He would walk into patient rooms and visit with people he didn't even know. He said he always felt better leaving than when he came. He had the freedom to come and go, but the people he visited didn't exactly have such freedom. Well, I suppose that's why I've always loved hospital visits.

Several years ago, I made such a visit. Ryan, a young man barely 20 was a college student who had recently graduated. He has an incredible voice to bless and entertain people. He collapsed and was rushed to the emergency room. Admitted to the hospital, they ran various tests. Nothing at first, but eventually there was a diagnosis of lymphoma.

I've prayed for him and sent well wishes but felt I was to visit Ryan one night. I had a photo of him I had taken at a concert when he was the featured soloist. It wasn't a great photo but I was able to make arrangements to have it framed. On the back of the photo, I attached my business card and wrote encouraging statements, then signed it and brought it with me to the hospital. Upon my arrival everyone at the nurse's station was friendly and a doctor personally escorted me to Ryan's room. He was shocked to see me. I gave him the photo and spoke words of faith for his healing and future. He loved the photo.

He was discharged the next day, but for that one night, it was just the two of us. I left his room feeling 10 feet tall. An investment of less than $10 brightened his evening and outlook. It was a tangible expression of care and concern which ended up meaning much to both of us.

Friend, we must be intentional when we bless people. Pour into their lives. Give of yourself.

JOB ON FRIENDSHIP

"After Job had interceded for his friends, God restored his fortune-and then doubled it! All his brothers and sisters and friends came to his house and celebrated. They told him how sorry they were, and consoled him for all the trouble God had brought him. Each of them brought generous housewarming gifts."
Job 42:10-11 (Message)

One of my favorite themes to talk about is friendship. A few years ago, I wrote an article on friendship. (Included later in this book.) One paragraph from that article struck me this morning:

*Friendship is essential for our emotional well-being. Without friends we drift in life's ocean, uncertain of our significance, and powerless to receive the instructions of others in our lives. Sometimes we settle for a life of seclusion instead of friendship. Joseph Addison (1672-1719) said "Friendship improves happiness, and abates misery, by doubling our joy, and dividing our grief."

I am convinced God wants us to have friends, be encouraged by our friends, and help our friends. In turn we will receive what we need. Job prayed for his friends and God restored to him — twice the amount of what he lost.

Instead of praying "God help me to sell my car" perhaps we should pray "God, help someone who needs a car to find the car I have for sale." Placing the emphasis on the needs of others is always better than praying selfish prayers.

May you be blessed with friends who love you, care for you, and as one friend of mine describes friendship: "holding the flashlight for you."

Holding the flashlight for you today my friend! I am very proud of you.

*The Hidden Value of Friendship
Thomas Harrison
© 1996, 2012, 2020

WHO HOLDS YOUR FLASHLIGHT?

Only my friend Scott and I know the details of this secret adventure. I have permission to tell the story with identifying details omitted.

Our mutual friend had been elected as the Senior Pastor of a small mission church. One Saturday we drove to the church to see the mission. A small sign identified the church, listing the previous pastor's name in adhesive metal letters. The kind one would purchase at a discount store.

The following Saturday well before daylight, we returned to the church. With letters and tools in hand, our goal was to update the church sign. We removed the previous pastor's name, cleaned the board, and installed the new name on both sides of the sign.

One held the flashlight, the other worked on the sign. We traded as we became tired. Holding the flashlight was no easy task—as one eye had to be on the work being performed—the other eye was on the lookout for law enforcement—or worse—a member of the church or the pastor.

Our clandestine operation was accomplished! As we drove away, we agreed neither would inform our friend of this act of service. We were overcome with God's blessing as we gave our gift in secret.

> *"Beware of practicing your righteousness before*
> *other people in order to be seen by them, for then you*
> *will have no reward from your Father who is in heaven…*
> *But when you give to the needy, do not let your left hand*
> *know what your right hand is doing, so that your giving may be*
> *in secret. And your Father who sees in secret will reward you."*
> Matthew 6:1, 3-4 (Phillips)

Who holds your flashlight? Who lends a hand when you have secret plans to help others? Who helps you while watching your back? I pray you have those kinds of friends—and you are one of those kinds of friends.

A HANDFUL OF FRIENDS

"I cannot even imagine where I would be today
were it not for that handful of friends who have given me a heart
full of joy. Let's face it, friends make life a lot more fun."
–Charles R. Swindoll

Several years ago, I was publicly acknowledged for earning my doctorate (Ph.D.) from Saint Louis University. It was a grand event. Friends and family came to celebrate this accomplishment with me.

Unfortunately, neither of my parents attended college. My father completed 8th grade, and my mother completed high school by correspondence while working on the family farm.

The first time I was in college, I dropped out to begin a career. So, it wasn't until the age of 30 that I completed my bachelor's degree at Oral Roberts University. I then went straight to graduate school, taking night classes to earn a master's degree from the University of Oklahoma.

All along my path, God placed friends and family who believed in me, and encouraged me to press on. Oh, how thankful I am for those wonderful people and their positive influence in my life!

My friend, let me encourage you to press on. What's the dream in your heart that you have never completed? Now is the time to start (or complete) that dream.

I believe in you!

FRIENDS HELP STEADY US

*"That you may be able to resist and stand your
ground on the evil day of danger, and, having done all the
crisis demands, to stand firmly in your place."*
Ephesians 6:13 (AMP)

Friends help us to stand when we need help. Several years ago, while working in my back yard, I broke my foot. Afterward, I used a cane to walk and held on to the wall to help steady me and keep my balance.

Friends help to form part of our balance, and support in life. Whether in person or by phone, text, tweet, chat, or post, our friends help us. Our friends help steady us and walk with us. They are our cane to help bear the burden, and reassure us as we walk.

Good friends tell us the truth, and give godly advice even when we don't wish to hear it.

Whatever you are facing today, know that God has placed friends in your life to bless, support, and encourage you.

Best blessings today, my friend. I am so proud of you.

DO YOU KNOW HOW TO TIE A TIE?

Several years ago, I was on assignment in Gadsden, Alabama. The day was filled with meetings and activities. I returned to my hotel and wanted a soft drink. I ventured into the convenience store across the highway to search for a local soft drink instead of the usual variety from a vending machine.

Leaving the convenience store, a tall, young man approached me. My first thought was: he wanted money. I heard "Excuse me, sir, may I ask you a question?" So, I was ready for the "I gave at the office" line. I replied, "Yes sir." His question: "Do you know how to tie a tie?"

I was stunned. This was either the most original line I'd ever heard or could he be serious? Of all people he was asking ME if I knew how to tie a tie.

"Yes, I know how to tie a tie. Why do you need to know?"

"Sir, I'm going to a funeral, and I want to show my respect by wearing a tie. I don't know how to tie one."

"You are going to a funeral *at night*?"

"Well, my grandmother just died. We are going to the funeral home to…"

"Oh, you are going to a visitation!"

"Yes, sir! Could you help me?"

I took his tie, tied it and helped the man with his collar and tie. He looked sharp. I told him I was sorry for his loss.

That encounter taught me much that night. Of all the people coming in and out of the convenience store, he asked *me* for help. I'm known for wearing ties. I have dozens of them and have owned and given away ties for years. Something I take for granted, he needed.

Gadsden, Alabama is a lot like other southern towns; filled with polite men whose parents taught them the value of respect. This man had meager means. His was not a designer tie made of silk. He knew wearing a tie demonstrated honor for the occasion and to the memory of his grandmother. That young man gave me —a total stranger — honor and respect by allowing me to be a part of the honor he planned to show in memory of his grandmother.

WISDOM IS BETTER THAN RUBIES

"For wisdom is better than rubies; and all the things that
may be desired are not to be compared to it. I wisdom dwell with
prudence, and find out knowledge of witty inventions."
Proverbs 8:11-12 (KJV)

May God grant you wisdom and witty inventions.

Let the creative flow from you: compose songs, write books, paint, draw, build, program, design, organize, tinker, restore, encourage, plan, invest, etc.

Your creative idea may be the miracle someone is praying for.

I am exceptionally proud of you, my creative friend; I believe you are full of wisdom.

THERE IS GREAT VALUE IN PREPARATION

"First plant your fields; then build your barn."
Proverbs 24:27 (Message)

Whatever you are building or tearing down you must first have a plan. If you are planning to fight or engaging in love or reconciliation; a plan is the first thing you need.

*"Champions do not become champions when
they win the event, but in the hours, weeks, months and years
they spend preparing for it. The victorious performance itself is
merely the demonstration of their championship character."*
–Alan Armstrong

*"Unfortunately, there seems to be far more opportunity
out there than ability… We should remember that good
fortune often happens when opportunity meets with preparation."*
–Thomas A. Edison

My friend, whatever you are going through, plan, prepare, and study. I have recently re-discovered the power in making a daily *To Do* list. This frees my mind from having to remember all which should be accomplished. I list errands, emails, telephone calls, tasks which must be performed.

Great satisfaction comes when I cross something off my list. At the end of the day, reviewing my list of accomplishments brings great peace.

Whatever you do, my friend--PLAN!

I am immeasurably proud of you today.

MONET DIDN'T COPY.
WE SHOULDN'T EITHER.

Several years ago, my wife and I toured with an orchestra of high school students on a ministry trip to France, Germany and Belgium. While in France, we visited the home and gardens of the famous painter Claude Monet (1840-1926). Monet established the Impressionism movement.

While reading about Monet, one statement struck me. In his early years, he would take his easel, canvas and supplies to the Louvre to paint. While at the Louvre, he saw other aspiring artists paint the masters' works in order to perfect their style.

Monet's approach was different as he looked out the windows of the Louvre and painted what he saw. He didn't copy the works of the masters; he created an entire movement based on the gift he was given. This reminds me of the book by John L. Mason: *You were born an original, don't die a copy!*

Whatever God has placed in your heart to do, GO! Do it now! We don't have to imitate others. We need to celebrate the gift God has given *us* — and be who we are created to be.

My friend, the time and hour are upon us — and upon you. Go! Do it now!

I am incredibly proud of you!

Mason, J. (1993). You're born an original, don't die a copy! Insight International.

Claude Oscar Monet biography | Life, paintings, influence on art | claudemonetgallery.org. (n.d.). Claude Oscar Monet - The Complete Works - claudemonetgallery.org. https://www.claudemonetgallery.org/biography.html

YOU ARE RICH IN BLESSINGS

*"The blessings of the Lord, it maketh rich,
and he addeth no sorrow with it."*
Proverbs 10:22 (KJV)

My friend, today may you know the blessing of God in every way.

The blessing of serving God and His people.

The blessing of family and friends.

The blessing of knowing your work matters to God.

The blessing of knowing you have done your best.

The blessing of a meal lovingly prepared by someone who loves you.

The blessing of rest and leisure.

The blessing of a clear conscience and a calm spirit.

The blessing of a good night's rest.

The blessing of the gift of another day to live and serve.

You are a blessing to so many. Enjoy this day of blessings!

BE THOU MY VISION

Be thou my vision, O Lord of my heart,
Be all else but naught to me, save that thou art;
Thou my best thought in the day and the night,
Both waking and sleeping, thy presence my light.

Be Thou My Vision
Dallan Forgall
Translator: Mary E. Byrne
(1905)

May this hymn become the cry of our heart today.

May God's vision for your life become abundantly
   clear to you.

May you sense God's presence today in a real way.

May you have a sense of your calling like never before.

As you serve people today and this week, may you
   encourage them.

May you stir within their hearts the desire to seek God.

May they understand the vision God has for their lives.

Hymnary.org is my primary research website for lyrics, author biography, and history of sacred music.

**"IN A WORLD FULL OF VERBAL VENOM;
MAY WE BE DISPENSERS OF PEACE,
LOVE, AND JOY."**

Dr. Thomas Harrison

WHY I BELIEVE IN DIVINE HEALING

*"Is anyone among you sick? Let him
call for the elders of the church, and let them
pray over him, anointing him with oil in
the name of the Lord. And the prayer of faith
willsave the one who is sick, and the Lord
will raise him up. And if he has
committed sins, he will be forgiven."*
James 5:14,15 (ESV)

*"But he was wounded for our transgressions;
he was crushed for our iniquities; upon him was the
chastisement that brought us peace,
and with his stripes we are healed."*
Isaiah 53:3 (ESV)

*"Bless the LORD, O my soul, and forget not all
his benefits, who forgives all your iniquity,
who heals all your diseases."*
Psalm 103:2,3 (ESV)

Years ago, I ministered on the subject *Why I believe in divine healing*. Here are some points from that message.

I believe in divine healing because:

I have experienced it. I have been with others at the moment they experienced it. As a baby, my wife was severely ill and could not gain weight. But she was miraculously healed!

Both Old and New Testaments record accounts of God's healing power and provision. Jesus taught about healing and performed great healing miracles. God has made it clear in both testaments that He does not change. (Malachi 3:6; Hebrews 13:8)

There has never been an era of time when divine healing was not needed. We need divine healing now and we will need it in the future as well.

Divine healing works with or without modern medicine and is not limited by medicine, doctors, or surgery. However, modern medicine itself is limited. Honest physicians admit that they often do not have answers to modern physical maladies. The source of all healing is God.

My friend, throughout our lives, we will have people asking us to pray for their healing. We should be ready with scriptures, and ready to pray the prayer of faith as described in the Bible.

Encourage your congregation to share testimonies of divine healing before prayer time in your church services. Encourage believers to journal and record their accounts of God's miracle provision of divine healing.

Praise God in advance for hearing our prayers and moving on our behalf.

GIVING AS WORSHIP

"Don't hoard your goods; spread them around.
Be a blessing to others. This could be your last night."
Ecclesiastes 11:2 (Message)

I have not always done this in my earlier years. A few years ago, I began to look at giving in a different way. It began to dawn on me that the penny I find in the parking lot could purchase one additional piece of literature for a missionary. The coffee I purchase for someone brings me one step closer to building a positive relationship. The meal I purchase in secret at a restaurant gives a lonely soul another reason, or perhaps the only reason to hope. The book I no longer need could become a treasure to a young minister.

I made a new commitment to recycling as giving.

Whatever we have, talent or treasure, let us be active in giving. Giving is another way we worship and serve God. Talent and treasure should be invested, recirculated, and compounded.

EARLY WILL I SEEK THEE OR UP ALL NIGHT

"0 God, thou art my God; early will I
seek thee: my soul thirsteth for thee."
Psalm 63:1 (KJV)

Several years ago, I interviewed former Rock and Roll musician-now pastor Mike Deasy. (He's famous. Google him!) He said of this verse that David, the musician, had been *jammin'* all night and was not an early riser.

On the other hand, before I was married, I worked the sign-on shift at a radio station which required me to leave the house at 3:30 a.m. In my view, there is something special about the early morning. Better to get your requests in before the rest of the world wakes up!

But whatever your preference, please know: God is near you and He is in the mood to hear from you. Late at night, early morning, or anywhere in between; He always wants to hear from you.

I am exceptionally proud of you!

AS WHITE AS THE COCONUT MEAT

*"Though your sins be as scarlet, they shall be as white as snow;
though they be red like crimson, they shall be as wool."*
Isaiah 1:18 (KJV)

I never see snow without thinking of the statesman missionary Ralph Hollandsworth. In his later years he helped me train many for the ministry.

He told the story of an American preacher coming to South Africa to minister to the masses and preaching with an interpreter. The minister used this verse in his sermon.

The translator asked Brother Hollandsworth how he should interpret the word "snow" to the people as the people had never seen snow, and had no idea what it was about. The veteran missionary said "preach it like it should be preached".

The translator told the masses: "though your sins be as scarlet, they shall be as white as the coconut meat ... "

The people responded to the translator's interpretation. The American minister left thinking his sermon on snow had great results.

Without understanding our audience, we communicate nothing. And sometimes those around us help us in ways we don't understand. Let us strive to understand our audience and appreciate those who labor with us.

May you be blessed today ... and consider the snow ... or the coconut meat.

"YOUR CREATIVE IDEA MAY BE THE MIRACLE SOMEONE IS PRAYING FOR."
Dr. Thomas Harrison

LIFE LESSON FROM A SALE BARN

As a young man, my grandfather was the wisest man I knew. Most summers my brother and I would spend a week or two on his farm in northwest Arkansas *helping*. One day, the three of us loaded goats into a truck to take them to the county sale barn. The goats were quite plentiful that year, and one can use only so many goats on a farm.

Sale barns were social events as well as a place to purchase livestock. As we entered the seating arena, I noticed an unusually dressed man who, in my pre-teenage mind looked rather odd and acted rather odd as well. I made an unkind and unflattering comment about this man. My grandfather gave me *the look*. He firmly told me "You know nothing about that man or his life. Be quiet." I realized I had invoked the correction of a man I adored. I was ashamed then, and now almost 50 years later I am embarrassed that my remarks about another life-traveler were unkind.

What seemed to be an endless parade of farm animals passed the auctioneer. Finally, grandfather's goats were on display. Bids rang out like popcorn exploding. When the gavel sounded, the successful bidder stood—it was THAT man.

I learned a valuable lesson that day. Judge no man; as he could be the one buying your grandfather's goats. Fortunately, this man never heard my words, neither did he know the life lesson he taught me that day at the sale barn.

"Do not judge by appearances,
but judge with right judgment."
John 7:24 (ESV)

Prejudice comes in all sizes, shapes, colors, and behaviors. While I have a finely defined belief system which governs my life, I have spent a lifetime trying to understand others who may be different.

PROVE THEM WRONG

You may know me as a pastor, television talk show host, radio announcer and voice over artist, or university professor and administrator, but here's my guilty little secret. One day in the seventh grade, I was taken from my regular class and placed in a group labeled "Remedial Reading." I was devastated. In my seventh-grade mind, the word "remedial" translated as "failure."

I couldn't wait to tell my mother about this injustice. Once home I poured my heart out with anger and embarrassment. My mother listened. I waited for her response. She said three little words which I've never forgotten: "Prove them wrong!"

The next day when it was my turn to read aloud, I gave it all I had. That was my last day in Remedial Reading. Those three powerful words have guided me for decades. "Prove them wrong" is the best answer to the accusers, doubters, and nattering nabobs.

My friend, the accuser of the brethren (Revelation 12:10) whispers and often shouts lies about you and me. Our character and integrity prove them wrong. Our steadfastness in faith proves them wrong. Our identification with Christ proves them wrong.

Whatever injustice, lie, or accusation which may come your way, I have three words for you:

Prove Them Wrong.

"May the Lord Jesus Christ and God our Father (who has loved us and given us unending encouragement and unfailing hope by his grace) inspire you with courage and confidence in every good thing you say or do."
2 Thessalonians 2:16 (Phillips)

God's best blessings be upon you today, and every day.

DINNER, LEFTOVERS, AND PLATES

My spiritual father, Rev. Ossie Jones told an amazing story from his childhood. During our 30+ year friendship I repeatedly asked him about this story and he told it often. The details never differed.

During the late 1920's or early 1930's, the Jones family lived in Oklahoma. Ossie's father was a pastor and served as the first full-time District Superintendent for the Oklahoma Assemblies of God. Times were tough and money, food, as well as employment were in short supply.

One evening the Jones family gathered around the table at the appointed time for dinner. Rev. Jones instructed everyone to bow their heads to offer thanks for the food. The problem was—there was no food on the table. There was literally nothing to eat and no funds to purchase any food.

During the prayer someone knocked on the door. Mrs. Jones went to the door while the prayer continued. Ossie was the youngest in the family, and confessed he peeked at what happened next. Unusually dressed people came into the home with plates of food—enough for several days. Oh my, how wonderful that food must have tasted!

After enjoying all the unexpected bounty, in typical Southern tradition Mrs. Jones washed the dishes and took them to the church with the expectation that their unexpected providers would return for their dishes. Time passed, yet the strangers never returned.

Months later, someone came to the church regarding a business matter and noticed the plates. Rev. Jones told the story of the evening prayer and miraculous supply of food delivered on these plates. The man informed Rev. Jones that these were no ordinary plates, but were in fact valuable antiques and immediately purchased them. Provision continued as the family used the money to purchase essentials. The Jones family continue to believe that the unusually dressed people were actually angels unexpectedly meeting their needs.

May we learn to believe for God's miraculous provision!

SIX CHARACTERISTICS OF GREAT PASTORS*

A Tribute to **Dr. Stan Toler**

My friend and fellow laborer in the Kingdom, Dr. Stan Toler, said great pastors share six characteristics:

- They know how to pray.
- They have personal integrity.
- They have great flexibility.
- They are team builders.
- They have a sense of direction.
- They have a great commitment.

Dr. Toler was a friend and client. We traveled together and he lived these traits both in public and private. While we were on the road, I learned it was his practice to call his congregation on birthdays, anniversaries, or to let them know he was praying for them.

He sent thousands of handwritten notes in his lifetime.

He was always giving.

Often, I would manage his book and product tables. I saw him give away scores of books. He encouraged us to give books to those who were reluctant or perhaps could not pay. He autographed books with the phrase "You are loved."

Stan Toler was a giant of a man who taught me much about life, business, ministry, and people. He knew people and wrote more than 100 books.

Dr. Toler was promoted to his heavenly reward November 18, 2017. You can read more about him at StanToler.com

Six Characteristics was originally written for pastors; however, all of us could benefit from striving for these qualities.

Book reflects pastor's work. (2017, May 19). StanToler.com. https://www.stantoler.com/articles/book-reflects-pastors-work/
*Used by permission Toler Leadership

THE HIDDEN VALUE OF FRIENDSHIP

There are great rewards in friendships. Many of us want to have friends and to be friends with those who are popular, exciting, and even influential. There are hidden values in friendships that transcend the 'act' of friendliness. This type of friendship is an authentic test of character and spiritual development.

I am convinced the saddest portion of scripture is John 5:7. "The impotent man answered him (Jesus), Sir, I have no man, when the water is troubled, to put me into the pool: but while I am coming, another steppeth down before me." (KJV).

In this passage, the afflicted man freely admits that he has no friends. He did not say his friends were out of town, at work, or running errands for him. He admitted the painful reality of his distress. He was friendless.

- Friendship is essential for our emotional well-being. Without friends we drift in life's ocean, uncertain of our significance, and powerless to receive the instructions of others in our lives. Sometimes we settle for a life of seclusion instead of friendship. Joseph Addison (1672-1719) said "Friendship improves happiness, and abates misery, by doubling our joy, and dividing our grief."

- Friendship heightens the creative talent in an individual. There is nothing like a compliment or a "pat on the back" to charge the creative drive within us. Dr. Paul Tournier suggests, "No one can develop freely in this world and find a full life without feeling understood by at least one person. Misunderstood, he loses his self-confidence, he loses his faith in life or even in God."

- Friendships lead to mentor relationships. Those who have mentors in their lives have "personal trainers" to help strengthen them. True mentor relationships must evolve over time, and may begin as friendships. Chesterfield, (1694-1773) said it best when he penned these words, "Real friendship is a slow grower, and never thrives unless engrafted upon a stock of known and reciprocal merit."

We all would do well to observe these three levels of friendship.

• Find someone older than you to serve as your spiritual mentor. This is one who will provide a mature voice and has the time and patience to help form you. In my teenage years, my grandfather shared some wisdom with me. He said, "Always make friends with old people. They will tell you everything they know." This wisdom has been with me for many years, and many friendships. My mentor has been working with me for nearly 25 years. Along with scripture and God's influence in my life, much of what you like in my life is a product of my mentor. He sharpens me, polishes me, and causes me to stretch personally and professionally.

• We all should develop a close friendship with one or two friends our own age, with whom we can share a good part of our experience. These friends are those in whom we confess our failures, temptations, wild ideas, and dreams. Friends our own age help us unwind by going to ball games together, or fishing, or in general spending time with us doing things we enjoy.

• Finally, let us recognize our potential to become another's mentor. Our professional and social circles may contain young "Timothys" who need to benefit from our wisdom. It was a moment of awakening when I first heard the words, "Thomas, you have become my mentor." What a responsibility! Given to me was the care and feeding of a friend who said, "I am granting you permission to pour into my life, and speak words of wisdom, correction and kindness."

Friendships take time. Relationships take even more time. Time, judiciously invested, increases the value of friendship. Make sure you invest your time only in those who do not abuse your time and talents.

Let us not be afraid to speak into someone's life. If the friendship develops, you will notice soon enough. If not, you have performed a kindness that pleases God. "The pleasantness of one's friend springs from his earnest counsel." Proverbs 27:9 (KJV). Someone is waiting for your friendship, counsel and mentorship.

©1996, 2012, 2020 Thomas Harrison

MOVE UP! DON'T GIVE UP!   87

How to Write Your Story

It occurs to me that reading this book may inspire you to write *your* story. But you may be saying to yourself, "I'm not a writer. I wouldn't know the first thing about how to put my story into words." While many people think that, in reality, you may know more about writing your story than you imagine.

If your children, grandchildren, niece, or nephew asked you to tell them a story, I have a feeling you would immediately oblige. Your mind would find some story or instance where something happened and relate it as excitingly and colorfully as possible. If the instance were one of a personal or spiritual nature, it would be flavored with emotion and zeal.

Consider these thoughts as you prepare for your journey:

We wish our ancestors would have written their stories.

_____

_____

_____

_____

Whatever your story, it deserves to be written and told.

_____

_____

_____

_____

Today, you can begin writing your story.

_____

_____

_____

_____

Let me help you outline your story. Consider the suggestions listed below to gather ideas for your story. It is acceptable to skip ones that may not apply, or if you don't have a thought at the moment. Writing is a process. Write some now. Leave it and let it percolate in your spirit. Return to the idea and add additional details, perspective, and link with a moral, scripture, or ideal.

Writing your story will help you heal and overcome challenges. Someone needs to read what you will soon write. When you have finished your story; write to me, I would love to read it!

I believe in you.

Dr. Thomas Harrison

Pray this prayer aloud in faith as you ask God for help in writing your story.

Father God, in the name of Jesus, I come to you today asking for your help[1]. After reading this book, Thomas Harrison has challenged me to begin writing my story. I confess to you; I need your help.

I want to write my story to bless my family and friends[2]. Please help me as I work through this process. Please guide me, Holy Spirit, to give me the pen (or keyboard) of a ready writer[3]. Unlock what holds me back and let the thoughts and words flow[4].

Oh God, help me tell the story without condemnation[5] or false emotions[6]. Please help me be free in my spirit to express my thoughts and ideas[7].

May honesty[8] and sincerity[9] abound as I write.

May you bring to my memory details, facts, and events that I may have forgotten[10].

Please help me to understand I do not have to be the hero in all of my stories[11]. We live in a fallen world[12], and often we have been the villain[13] in a circumstance, yet we have learned divine truth once the event has transpired.

May I be humble and gentle in my writing[14] while being bold in proclaiming the truth[15] you have given me.

Help me realize that sharing my testimony builds faith in my own life and spirit[16], as it also encourages others[17]. The ultimate goal of my testimony is to give you praise, oh God, for your goodness[18].

Thank you, God, for hearing[19] and answering my prayer[20,] and moving on my behalf[21].

Thank you, God, for helping me to write as you inspire me[22]. In the holy and mighty name of Jesus, I pray.

Amen

Look up the scriptures noted in the above prayer. Read them in various translations and make notes in the back of this book. Let these scriptures come to life in your spirit as you write your story.

1. James 1:5

2. Deuteronomy 31:19, Proverbs 3:3

3. Psalm 45:1

4. Psalm 147:18, John 7:38

5. Romans 8:1

6. James 1:8

7. Proverbs 8:12

8. 1 Timothy 2:2

9. 2 Corinthians 1:12, Titus 2:7

10. John 14:26

11. Micah 6:8

12. Romans 5:12

13. Psalm 106:6, 1 John 1:10

14. Proverbs 15:1, James 3:17, 2 Timothy 2:24

15. Proverbs 28:1, Ephesians 3:12,

16. 2 Timothy 1:8

17. Psalm 19:7

18. Psalm 50:23

19. 1 John 5:14-15, Jeremiah 29: 12, 13, John 14:13

20. John 16:24, Luke 11:10, Matthew 7:11

21. Psalm 68:19, Philippians 1:6

22. Habakkuk 2:2

Memorable Life Events

_____

_____

_____

_____

Quotes, Sayings, Expressions of Speech

_____

_____

_____

_____

People who have inspired you

_____

_____

_____

_____

News events that have inspired you

_____

_____

_____

_____

Unusual life occurrences

_____

_____

_____

_____

Scriptures that have inspired you

_____

_____

_____

_____

Travel that has inspired you

_____

_____

_____

_____

Awards, Recognition, Certification, training you have received

_____

_____

_____

_____

Military service

_____

_____

_____

_____

Employment, Moonlighting, Part-Time Employment

_____

_____

_____

_____

Stories you have heard from family and friends which have inspired you

_____

_____

_____

_____

What do you wish your family knew about you?

_____

_____

_____

_____

Times when you were not the hero of your own story

_____

_____

_____

_____

Titles for your stories

_____

_____

_____

_____

(Consider catchy phrases, unusual sequences
of words, alliteration, humor or emotion)

NOTES

_____
_____
_____
_____
_____
_____
_____
_____
_____
_____
_____
_____
_____
_____
_____
_____
_____
_____
_____
_____
_____
_____
_____
_____
_____
_____

NOTES

NOTES

_____

_____

_____

_____

_____

_____

_____

_____

_____

_____

_____

_____

_____

_____

_____

_____

_____

_____

_____

_____

_____

_____

_____

_____

_____

_____

_____

_____

It is Time for Your Story!

I trust you have enjoyed *Move Up! Don't Give Up!* Perhaps these stories have provided encouragement and inspiration.

Would you consider sharing a copy of *Move Up, Don't Give Up* with your family or pastor?

I welcome the opportunity to tell these and other stories yet to come with your church, Bible study, corporate meeting, or training event.

Perhaps these stories have inspired you to look for your own and begin writing and sharing stories with your family and friends.

If you would like to share your stories with me, I would love to read them. A sequel could contain stories from my family, friends, and extended family—you!

Here is how to contact me:

Dr. Thomas Harrison
7107 South Yale Avenue
Suite 337
Tulsa, Oklahoma 74136-6308
918.585.5333
ThomasMyFriend@aol.com

P.S.: Among the most enjoyable parts of my week are the occasions when Jasmine and I roam on our *adventures*. Before you ask, the answer is Yes! Yes, I tell stories to Jasmine the Wonder Dog. There is one I tell her about how she is the bravest dog in the universe. That one is *mostly* true.

REFERENCES

I have been enriched by working with scores of gifted and God-anointed people who have changed my life. While it is impossible and impractical to list all of them, I thought you would enjoy knowing these people and their products and services.

The following pages are a tribute to these friends, as they have helped me become the person I am today.

Inclusion in this section is solely at the author's discretion. Financial consideration was neither extended nor accepted. No warranties are expressed or implied.

When You Lose Someone You Love
20th Anniversary Edition

Written as a series of heart-to-heart letters, best-selling author Richard Exley draws on years of pastoral ministry to give you the comfort of a true friend. You'll draw reassurance from the real experiences of others who have faced devastating loss, and begin to see how hope can one day triumph over grief. Most importantly, you will discover how the mercy and grace of God provide the promise of eternal life.

Your most difficult questions -- including your doubts about God's goodness, or perhaps His very existence, are fearlessly addressed. Realistic and empathetic insights will enable you to trust God with your loss even though it seems to make no sense.

Long after the flowers have faded and the sympathy cards are tucked away, "When You Lose Someone You Love" will still be speaking peace and promise to your heart. An expression of continuing concern and comfort, it is sure to be your most welcome companion during your journey through grief.

Order from the author:
RichardExleyMinistries.org

KC Photography

I pray that God continues to use me to bless others with my passion for capturing my clients' precious moments.

I am very thankful to be able to capture special moments for Dr. Thomas Harrison. He is a dear friend to my family, I am grateful for his continuous words of wisdom and prayers.

Christina Bullard
KC Photography
Muskogee, Oklahoma
kcphotography918@yahoo.com

Learn to pray with authority. Develop personal disciplines.
Practice spiritual habits. Grow your faith in GOD.
Live your Christianity in practical ways.

Myles Holmes is a gifted communicator, author, television host, and pastor. He hosts multiple social media outlets, including "Battle of the Republic" with more than 84,000 followers.

Myles has more than 2.1 million followers on Facebook.

Available through Amazon

oasisnetwork.org

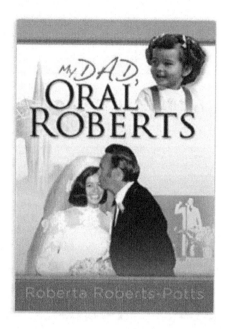

My Dad, Oral Roberts
Roberta Roberts Potts

He was born at the height of the War to End All Wars, in the little town of Ada, Oklahoma. By the time Oral Roberts passed from this life in 2009, American evangelicalism became a truly global endeavor, due in no small part to this faith-healer who began his ministry in tent revivals.

Now, his daughter, Roberta Roberts Potts has penned a loving, inside view of the man and his ministry. Filled with anecdotes and observations about one of the world's most famous preachers, *My Dad, Oral Roberts* serves as the only biography of Granville Oral Roberts from his family.

Full of wonderful photos and memories—both poignant and happy—*My Dad, Oral Roberts* is a truly fascinating read, and a wonderful testament to a life of faith.

Order from the author:
www.robertapotts.com/my-book/

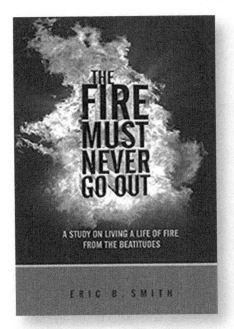 

Eric B. Smith
Pastor and Author

The Fire Must Never Go Out: "Keeping the flame of the Lord burning brightly is the mandate of each and every believer. In this practical study, the words of Jesus in the Beatitudes are examined closely revealing powerful steps for maintaining the fire of God in our lives."

God Card: "Learning to hear and follow God's voice accurately is both a lifetime pursuit and a spiritual skill that must be developed. In The God Card you will learn the pathway to better hearing and discernment of God's voice in your life."

Available through Amazon

The Fire Must Never Go Out

The God Card

FREE LEADERSHIP RESOURCES

www.StanToler.com

Made in the USA
Monee, IL
17 July 2021

73296974R00069